What People Are Saying About HIS Advocates...
Testimonials

"I came to HIS Advocates in search of an exit strategy, both from the corporate structures I'd faithfully served for nearly two decades and from a church system that felt equally constrained, where the Scriptures were rarely taught faithfully and the gospel was watered down into a feel-good punchline that left me hungering for the whole truth. As a Marine Corps and Iraq War veteran and former government contractor in Diplomatic Security, the DOJ, DOE, Treasury, and DoD, with top-secret clearances and frontline experience in Iraq, I have seen firsthand how deeply the corporate model has infiltrated these institutions. Yet nothing prepared me for the spiritual awakening that began when I discovered HIS Advocates in 2018.

Through the Living-in-the-Private Program, I learned to reclaim my identity as a State Citizen under God, not a corporate "U.S. citizen." Under Kelby Smith's mentorship, he's more than a guide; he's family, godfather to my children, and a brother in the faith. I found both the practical tools and the spiritual refuge I'd been longing for. Kelby is exactly who he says he is: a man of integrity whose ministry has delivered nothing but victories in my life.

Today, I walk free of the statutory entanglements that once bound me, and though it has not always been easy, I am standing firm on God and holding fast to His truth. If you're questioning your place in this world or wondering if true freedom is possible, I encourage you to accept Kelby's challenge: go deeper, root yourself in God's word, and let HIS Advocates guide you home. I give all glory and honor to YAH for his newfound freedom because He alone makes us free.

Now unto the King eternal, immortal, invisible, the only wise God, be honour and glory for ever and ever. Amen. 1 Tim 1:17. KJV"

- **Ebiezer son of Rito**
Ambassador and Witness to Christ

'Truth is often elusive and even harder to accept when it challenges everything we've been taught.

As a physician with over 30 years of experience, I once believed that education, textbooks, and academic systems were the foundations of truth and success. Over time, I came to realize how deeply misled we've been. What I thought was knowledge turned out to be carefully curated information, designed more to condition than to empower.

That's when Kelby Smith entered my life.

Over the past several years, Kelby has walked beside me, providing insight, clarity, and unwavering support. He has opened my eyes to a deeper understanding of who we truly are, where we've come from, and how much of the world around us operates behind a veil of illusion. Through his guidance, I have been able to strengthen and secure my personal and family situation in ways I never imagined possible.

Because of Kelby, my focus on faith, family, fitness, and the future has taken on a new level of clarity and purpose. His unique talents, deep convictions, and uncompromising values have not only elevated my understanding, they've fueled a transformation in how I approach my work and those I serve each day.

Kelby has been more than a mentor; he's been a catalyst for spiritual, intellectual, and practical growth.

With sincere gratitude,

- **Dr. Mark Hepp, M.D.**

"My journey with HIS Advocates, s.s.m. began while trying to assist my Pastor with securing a religious property-tax exemption for our assembly. One of the members introduced me to the concept of a Self-Supported Ministry (SSM), and that led me to the work of Kelby Smith. I remember telling Pastor, "I think I found something." Pastor responded, "You go first. Check it out. If it bears fruit, I'll follow your lead." I wasn't just dealing with a tax issue; I was in the midst of a divorce, had lost all my children, and was awakening to how entangled we truly are in this legal system. HIS Advocates didn't just offer solutions for religious exemption; they offered a clear, lawful path to freedom.

What made HIS Advocates, s.s.m. different was the structure, precision, and support. Kelby's team provided a powerful diagram and step-by-step documentation to unravel the binding contracts that most of us never knowingly entered into: birth certificates, marriage licenses, driver's licenses, voter registration, and more. The program required commitment, but the legwork was clear: send the letters, follow the process, and stay the course. HIS Advocates took care of the templates, affidavits, and guidance, helping me to not only understand the system but to walk out of it lawfully, with confidence and peace of mind.

Today, by the grace of the Most High YAH, I no longer pay income tax, property tax, or sales tax. I live free without fear of legal attacks or government intrusion into my household. It was under the leadership of my Pastor and through the example of his ministry that I first heard the call to come out of her, my people. HIS Advocates, s.s.m. became the practical tool YAH used to help me fulfill that call lawfully and completely. Kelby Smith and his team didn't just teach theory; they helped me live it. This ministry has become a vessel that YAH is using to help the remnant truly come out of her."

- Kabeer Gbaja-Biamila
Elder, Retired NFL Hall of Famer Green Bay Packers

"I would love to tell the whole God story of how I ended up working with Kelby and HIS Advocates, but there might not be enough room. It was truly a divinely orchestrated event. That said, Kelby and his team were instrumental and continue to be instrumental in walking my husband

and me through this complex, yet amazing process of accessing true freedom. It is truly a complete mindset shift; once you know the truth, you can't unknow it, therefore you find that you must act upon it or let it eat away at your consciousness until you answer the call.

My husband and I answered the call and stepped in, yet we would have had no clue about anything involved in this process of "unplugging" from the system and "plugging" into true freedom. Kelby has crafted an amazing system of training and education that is unmatched by anything else I have seen. I admire his humility and rely upon his confidence to continue to inspire me to educate myself and fight for truth by taking the actions necessary to walk the talk. I am so glad that God led me to Kelby and HIS Advocates. I feel it has empowered me to honor God with my allegiance to the Kingdom and has given me a tangible process to carry that out. Blessings."

- Jamie Kliewe
OMNI Health Ministries

I've had the privilege of knowing Kelby Smith for nearly three decades. In that time, he has proven to be not only a trustworthy friend but a true brother in Christ whose passion for truth and liberty is unwavering.

As the founder of SB Salt and Light Ministries, a home-based Christian outreach including a blog, weekly Bible studies, and multiple prayer conference calls, I've encountered my share of challenges. In 2010, I faced a serious issue when my bank unlawfully froze my personal funds. Kelby personally guided me through the process of drafting a powerful, legally sound letter to the institution. Within days of receiving it, the bank lifted all holds on my account.

That pivotal moment opened the door for a greater journey. Kelby later helped me establish a Self-Supporting Humanitarian Foundation, allowing me to operate securely and privately ever since. I've had peace of mind and no further issues, thanks to the guidance and private education offered through HIS Advocates.

I wholeheartedly recommend HIS Advocates to anyone seeking to live privately, reclaim their rights, and operate with integrity outside of oppressive systems. It's more than an organization, it's a movement rooted in truth, faith, and freedom.

In His Service,

- Skip Barland
SB Salt and Light Ministries

"When I was young, I learned about the men who founded our country and their desire and intention to be free in a nation built on personal liberty. I matured and as I looked around me, I saw few instances of people living in freedom or possessing personal liberty! I could sense there was a problem but could not grasp exactly how we the people were losing our freedoms. About ten years ago I found the answer to that question by signing up for a one-month free membership with HIS Advocates! I was elated to also discover, through my membership, the solutions to regaining and protecting our original freedoms. I now live as a free man in America, just as the founders had envisioned, I live free in the private. Through my His Advocate membership I learned the difference between public and private in very concrete terms and now consider Living-in-the-Private to be a blessing from God shed upon "we the People."

I remain a member of HIS Advocates all these years later and I am incredibly grateful that I was led to explore the education this faith-based ministry provides! Not only do their resources provide the necessary information to achieve freedom, but the Living-in-the-Private Program also offers assistance in completing the required documents to regain your freedom and maintain a status as a free man or woman living a life of liberty. Additionally, there is ongoing support regarding exactly how to maintain yourself and all your affairs in the private.

Through my HIS Advocates membership, I have obtained a passport as a State Citizen with all rights and protections afforded to Americans, corrected my political status with all government agencies, resolved tax issues, attempted garnishments and multiple other issues with agencies attempting to intrude upon my liberties and as of this writing I have been successful in every such endeavor. All these issues to date and more have been resolved in my favor due to the support provided by HIS Advocates.

My experience with Kelby Smith and the team at HIS Advocates has been 100% positive. They are always helpful and professional. When communicating with the team, I have been continually impressed by the integrity of the team members and their true desire to help all who are interested to become free. I offer my highest recommendation for Kelby Smith, HIS Advocates, and the God loving people associated with this ministry."

- Jim Westmoreland
L.Ac., NMT, Diplomate NCCAOM

I've had the privilege of knowing Kelby Smith for over 13 years, and in that time, his influence on my life has been nothing short of transformative. Through HIS Advocates, Kelby has helped reshape my understanding of freedom, identity, and spiritual alignment. His guidance has empowered me to live with clarity, purpose, and integrity—

not just to exist in this world, but to engage with it from a place of truth and conviction.

Imagine having a company that operates 100% outside the jurisdiction of any agency. Kelby's work has profoundly impacted not only my life and the lives of my family but also the lives of countless individuals across the nation and around the globe. I am deeply proud of our friendship and inspired by the mission of HIS Advocates. Their commitment to education, empowerment, and spiritual grounding continues to make a lasting difference for so many.

Daniel Brigman
Numanna Foods

Kelby Smith is a powerful force in the freedom movement. For decades, I have been aware of the deception with the Federal tax system and have done my best to navigate around it. All along, I knew that I would find the right support that came in the community of HIS Advocates, and Kelby Smith is the steady hand guiding it.

I have encountered individuals who take advantage of people seeking legitimate solutions. Kelby is different. His unwavering commitment to truth and spiritual alignment sets him apart. His leadership offers real clarity in a sea of confusion. He is a true beacon of light, helping others chart a safe and real path to lasting freedom.

I thank God for Kelby Smith and the HIS Advocates community. They are an answer to prayer.

- Joey Soto
Vital Variegation

HIS Advocates, s.s.m.

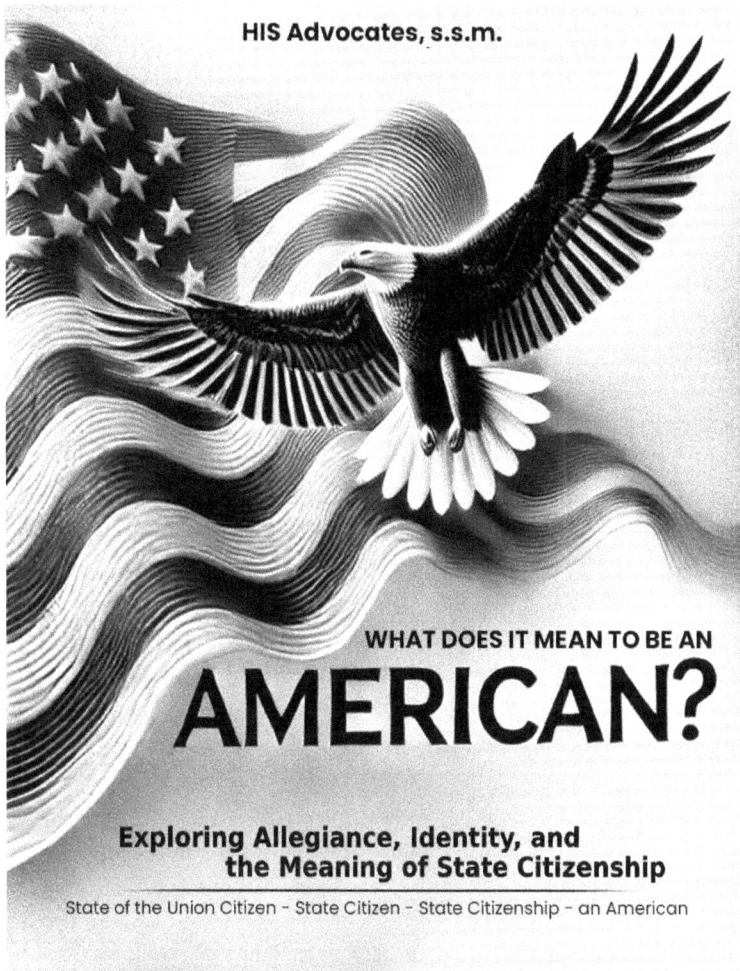

WHAT DOES IT MEAN TO BE AN

AMERICAN?

Exploring Allegiance, Identity, and the Meaning of State Citizenship

State of the Union Citizen - State Citizen - State Citizenship - an American

DISCLAIMER: This publication is for informational and educational purposes only.
It reflects the author's good-faith opinions, interpretations, and historical discussions at
the time of writing. Readers are encouraged to conduct their own research and
independently verify all citations and assertions. The availability and content of external
resources are subject to change.

Nothing in this book should be construed as legal, financial, or other professional
advice, and readers should seek private counsel before taking any action based on the
material presented.

While reasonable efforts have been made to ensure accuracy and integrity, the content is
provided "as is," without warranties of any kind, express or implied. Laws, regulations,
and policies vary by jurisdiction and may change without notice; examples are
illustrative and may not fit your circumstances.

The authors and contributors do not advocate unlawful conduct, evasion of lawful
obligations, or resistance to valid legal authority. Any interpretation or use of this
material contrary to applicable law is solely the responsibility of the reader.

To the fullest extent permitted by law, the authors, publishers, and affiliated
organizations disclaim liability for any loss, injury, or adverse consequence arising from
the use or misuse of the information contained in this publication.

This book is dedicated to you!

The seeker, the wanderer, the one who always knew something wasn't right. To the soul who feels the weight of unseen chains but has never stopped searching for the key. To the ones who will read these pages with tears in their eyes and truth burning in their hearts.

To those who were born for more, but needed permission to believe it.

To every future member of HIS Advocates who will rise from confusion into clarity, from bondage into liberty.

May you know that GOD has always been guiding you, just as He guided me. He is not just the Author of liberty, but the very breath of it. He placed people in your path, just as He did in mine. He orchestrated divine appointments, hidden revelations, and unlikely messengers to lead you back to your rightful inheritance.

You are not crazy. You are not alone. You are waking up.

May this book be the trumpet blast that shakes your soul awake and breaks every lie that has held you back.

May it lead you home, to who you truly are, to whose you truly are, and to the freedom that has always been yours.

This is your turning point. This is your moment.

Welcome to the journey. Welcome to HISAdovcates.

Welcome home.

Acknowledgements

First and foremost, all glory and honor belong to GOD.

It was GOD who opened the gates to the ancient paths, making divine introductions to men who held keys to unlock the truth about State Citizenship and the Republic. It was GOD who appointed every moment, curated every piece of data, every case citation, and every legal document I would one day need, not just to understand the mission, but to carry it. HIS fingerprint was on every page before I ever set pen to paper.

When I stood before the DEPARTMENT of STATE, met with skepticism and resistance, it was GOD who gave me the precise words to speak—words that silenced opposition and lit the path forward for countless others to follow. HIS voice rang louder than fear, and HIS authority carried greater weight than any bureaucratic gatekeeper.

HIS Advocates was not built by the hands of men. GOD built the foundation. GOD formed the team. GOD established the vision. Every soul that has come through the doors of this ministry was first led by HIS Spirit.

To Don Mago, my brother and friend: Thank you for disobeying me when I needed it most. When I told you to get back to work, you looked me in the eye and said, "No. You're going to this seminar." You saw something I could not. That one decision…your refusal to let me shrink back, altered the entire course of my life. Because of you, I walked into a room that changed everything.

To my mother: Your faith, your strength, and your unwavering support in my earliest years, and in the fragile beginning of this great mission, have never gone unnoticed. You believed in me when all I had was an idea and a prayer. You breathed life into both.

To Derek Carrington: When I had lost everything, when the world turned its back, you stepped in without hesitation. You gave not just your finances, but your heart. You believed in the vision before there was even a blueprint. You made sure I got to the place where truth would finally find me. I can never repay what you've done, but I pray the fruit of this mission is a small return on the seeds you sowed.

To everyone reading this: This book is not just a publication. It is a lifeline, a testimony, and a wake-up call. May these pages tear down lies, resurrect purpose, and lead you to a deeper truth, not just about what it means to be an American, but what it means to be free under God.

From the depths of my soul,

Thank you.

Kelby Smith
Founder, HIS Advocates.

Table of Contents

Prologue

———————— ❈ ————————

Have you ever had that nagging feeling, deep in your gut, that things just don't add up?

That maybe, just maybe, you've been lied to? If you've spent any time really paying attention to what's going on in this country, you can't help but notice it. The darkness, deception, and a creeping sense that the America you grew up believing in no longer exists. Anybody out there old enough to remember the '50s and early 60's when everybody drove convertibles and left their key in the ignition most of the time? The "Land of the Free? Home of the Brave"? Yeah, right. It feels more like we're being herded, controlled, and manipulated by forces we can't quite see, but feel every day.

Like many of you, I've been on my own journey in business and life. The more I started thinking logically about the events that shaped our world, the more questions I began to ask: **big questions,** questions that once you began asking, everything began to change.

9/11/2001

I remember 9/11 like it was yesterday. I was at home in Corona, California. I had an infant son, and my daughter was just two days away from being born. It was one of my life's most surreal and emotionally charged weeks. Patriotism surged in the aftermath. I couldn't believe that I saw the buildings fall straight out of the sky. First, a massive fire, followed by explosions, and then… a sense of unity. It felt pure at first. However, over time, it started to feel like something else. Something dark. I wanted to believe in my country's leaders, to trust their narrative, but the more I dug, the less it made sense. That's when I stumbled upon a documentary film called "Loose Change." Let me tell you…If you haven't seen it yet, you need to. It pulls back the curtain on the 9/11 story we were all fed, and when you start verifying the details, the cracks in the official narrative are impossible to ignore.

Now, don't get me wrong, this book isn't about rehashing 9/11 conspiracies; however, that moment in time was life-changing and truth-telling. What they tried to use to bind us lit a fire in me. They wanted to control us and use our patriotism against us. Instead, they sparked a movement of people who dared to question everything.

Once your eyes are opened, there's no going back.

Fast-forward a few years. I owned a mortgage company with hundreds of loan officers, riding the ups and downs of the California market. I watched something that shook me to my core: Treasury Secretary Henry Paulson was on his knees, literally **begging Nancy Pelosi for an $800 BILLION bailout** (they could have paid off every house that was in foreclosure at the time and offered them a low-interest-rate loan directly). It wasn't just shocking, it was insulting. It was an obvious farce played out right in front of us, and they expected us to buy it! Grown men don't do business that way. It was pure theater. The more I thought about it, the more disgusted I became. That money, actually our money, didn't go where it should have gone. It bypassed the people who actually needed help and instead went straight to the banks. And, guess what? To this day, much of that money has never been repaid. It was a scam, plain and simple.

At that point, I knew something was deeply wrong with the United States. We're not the self-governed, free-spirited people our Founding Fathers envisioned. We are pawns controlled by a small evil group of men and women who believe they are above us, who manipulate the system for their own gain.

That realization led me deeper down the rabbit hole. A friend of mine, "Don," pushed me to attend a seminar, which, at the time, I thought would be a waste of my weekend. However, it turned out to be the wake-up call I needed. What I learned reshaped my entire understanding of what this country really is, and more importantly, what it isn't. The United States isn't the beacon of freedom we've been led to believe. The United States is a corporation run by a few super-rich aristocrats and designed to keep the rest of us in line. What's worse, it is a corporation that is not only in bankruptcy but also insolvent, with the people and assets of the United States of America placed in receivership without our knowledge.

I started connecting the dots, and the picture that emerged was horrifying. We're living in a system that's rigged against us! From the taxes we pay to the education our children receive, everything is designed to keep us subdued and subservient to a global agenda. Here's the kicker: it's all out in the open if you're willing to look. The symbolism, the secret societies, the wealthy families that pull the strings…it's all there to see. They've orchestrated a system that funnels power and wealth to the few, while the rest of us are left fighting for scraps.

A Conspiracy Isn't a 'Conspiracy Theory' Once It's Proven True

Call it a conspiracy if you want, but ask yourself this: What's more likely? That we're all just imagining this massive, interconnected web of deceit? Or, that we're finally waking up to a truth that they never wanted us to see?

The truth is, they've built a machine to strip us of our freedoms, to mold us into something we were never meant to be... slaves to the "global economy." Once you see it, you can't unsee it. We've been taxed into oblivion, forced to watch the fruit of our labor being siphoned away. Then we're told to be grateful for the scraps they let us keep. No matter how many ways they try to sugarcoat it, it is tyranny.

Our forefathers fought a revolution against this kind of oppression. They bled for the right to be free men and women, and to be governed by a Republic, built on God's law and individual liberty. What we have now is a hollow shell of that vision. It's become a twisted and corrupted version by those **who seek to control rather than to serve.**

The law, God's law, still rules supreme, and there's a way out. In this book, we're going to **pull back the curtain** on the lies you've been told, the **hidden systems that are in place to keep you in slavery, and** reveal the path to true freedom. Once you know the truth, you'll have the power to reclaim what's rightfully yours.

Intrigued? Keep Reading – This is just the beginning.

So, what does all of this have to do with State Citizenship?

Everything...

L et me explain.

Like many of you, I went down the rabbit hole. I had to know more about what the media wouldn't tell us. That's when I started looking into the law. I'm talking about real law. The kind of law found in Supreme Court rulings, Black's Law Dictionary, case precedents, and legal structures that have been deliberately buried or obscured for decades. What I discovered shocked me. It was more than just a conspiracy theory. It was conspiracy fact. It was a cold and hard truth. It was more real than anything I could ever have imagined.

The real question is *why*? Why would those in power go to such lengths to suppress this knowledge; this idea of state sovereignty, the notion that you can actually be self-governed, not under the thumb of a corporate crime syndicate masquerading as the United States government? Why create these phony, derogatory terms like "sovereign citizen" to make anyone who dares question the system sound like a lunatic? The answer is clear. They don't want us to realize that we can free ourselves, not just as individuals, but as a nation. Because the minute we wake up to this reality, their control over us disappears.

Control: That's The Key.

Take a look at what Klaus Schwab, the founder and former head of the World Economic Forum, has been telling us for years: *"You will own nothing, and you will be happy."* Really? That is their plan...a system of global domination in which a few control the many, and we the people are nothing more than tiny cogs in their machine. They've been testing that plan for years. Remember the "plandemic?" It was the ultimate litmus test to see who would comply and who would resist. And sadly, many fell in line.

I have to admit, even I had a weak moment. I walked into a Costco one day with a mask half on. I was tired of fighting with the security guards and the managers. I was tired of asking them to show me the contract that gave them the authority to force me to wear a mask. Shortly after I had reached my limit of frustration, I got a call from a good friend, a man I had helped break free from this system years ago. He lit into me. "You will stand for all of us as you did before," he said. "You will not wear that mask. You will go into that store and buy your food like a free man." You know what? He was right. I went back in without a mask and my head held high. Sure, they tried to stop me, but I wasn't having it as I knew the law and my rights. On that very same day, I walked through the store as if it were my personal shopping experience. They practically gave me concierge service.

Here's the point...it wasn't just about the mask, it was about power! Power not only comes from knowing who you are and standing up for what you believe in, while knowing what's right, reasonable, and prudent, while understanding the law. If you know the law and your rights as a State Citizen, you realize that they don't get to decide anything.

The law, the actual law, still stands, even if they try to pretend it doesn't. Understand that, and the fear disappears.

By the time all this happened, I had been a State Citizen for years. It wasn't just something I believed in…it was something I lived. Let me tell you, knowing the law gave me the confidence to fight back against the oppression we've all been feeling. "Life, liberty, and the pursuit of happiness" aren't just words, they're a call to action, and they demand sacrifice. I pledged my time and energy to stand against a system that wants to crush our spirit. The more I dug, the more I discovered about their plans for global control, and about how deep this rabbit hole really goes. I also learned something else. I found out that I could no longer be classified as a debtor, as a mere "U.S. Citizen" beholden to a bankrupt corporation.

I realized that, in the end, both man's law and God's law have my back. If the day ever comes when everything falls apart, I know that I'm not just a victim of this broken system…I'm a creditor under God, someone who has rights and protections that can never be taken away.

Keep reading, and you will discover the same thing. You'll learn how to stand tall as a free American, not beholden to any corporation, government, or false authority. The truth is here, and it's time we all learn to see it.

Stay with me, we're just getting started.

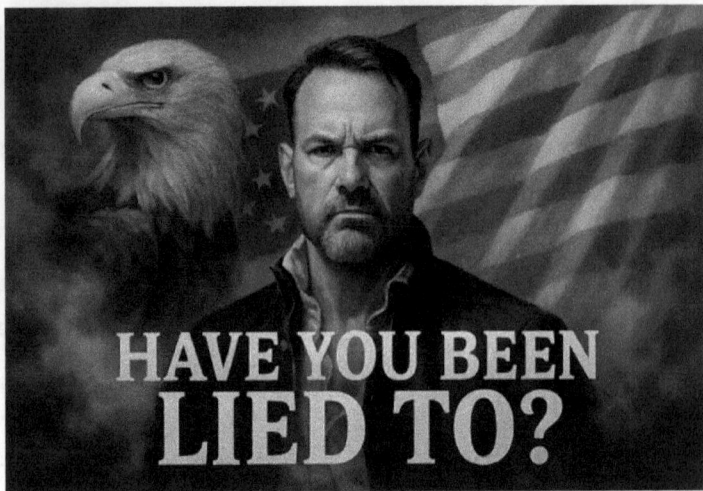

HAVE YOU BEEN
LIED TO?

CHAPTER 1

State of the Union Citizenship vs. U.S. Citizenship: Which Holds More Weight in America?

Why State Citizenship?

O ur unalienable (un-a-lien-able) rights come from God, not the government, and our allegiance should always be to Him. This foundational truth frames our thoughts as a state Citizens. God is the true Sovereign and we are subject to Him alone.

This white paper aims to provide a high-level overview of state Citizenship and clarify the distinction between a citizen of a state and a federal citizen (aka U.S. Citizen or 14th Amendment citizen). The importance of this distinction cannot be overstated. State Citizenship reflects the original intent of America's founders, and the sovereignty of the states, rooted in the rights of the People as the sovereigns. Let's take a chronological walk for truth.

Foundational Principles of Citizenship in America (1776–1887)

The Declaration of Independence (1776)

Our declaration begins with: **"The unanimous Declaration of the thirteen united States of America."** Here, "united" is lowercase, indicating that the states were distinct political entities that voluntarily united for a common cause. This would also imply that "united" is also an adjective that describes a people united and coming together under a "trust indenture" called the Declaration.

We also see that it declared the colonies as "free and independent states," emphasizing that the rights of the people come from their Creator, not from government itself. The phrase, "endowed by their Creator with certain unalienable Rights", emphasizes the divine origin of these rights. The question that naturally follows is this: **What is the nature of the "STATE" as we know it today, compared to the "state" envisioned at the founding?** Has the organic, sovereign community of self-governing Citizens been replaced by a statutory construct? In other words: Have our autonomous states become mere federal subdivisions inhabited not by sovereigns, but by subjects defined as "persons" under administrative law? See the Key Terms Section in the Index for – state vs. STATE vs. Federal State.

The Articles of Confederation (1777, ratified 1781)

Under the Articles of Confederation, Article I states: "The Stile of this Confederacy shall be 'The United States of America.'" Here we find one of the **first official uses of "United States" as a proper noun, and it refers to the confederation of states, not a single national government with supremacy over the states.**

Article IV established the principle of "free inhabitants" and recognized the unique sovereignty of each state to define its own citizens' rights. **The Articles reinforced that each state retained its independence**, with the federal government serving only in a limited role. (in service to the states)

The Constitution of the united States of America (1787, ratified 1789)

The Preamble to the Constitution opens with "We the People of the United States, in Order to form a more perfect Union." Here, we see that it was the people, the Citizens of the states, coming together to form a limited federal government. The "United States" appears formally as a proper noun, but the context suggests a compact between sovereign states forming a limited federal structure, not a consolidated national government.

The Constitution further emphasized state sovereignty. Article IV, Section 2 states: **"The Citizens of each State shall be entitled to all Privileges and Immunities of Citizens in the several States,"** ensuring that state Citizenship was foundational, with no mention of federal or national citizenship.

The Bill of Rights (1791)

It's important to understand that the **Bill of Rights was intended for the federal government; it restricted federal power, not state power.** This reinforced the understanding that states are independent sovereigns in most matters, except in matters in which they have ceded authority–specifically in situations in which states have given the federal government limited enumerated powers. Essentially, the federal government only has the powers explicitly granted to it by the states from the Constitution, while all other powers remain with the states and the People.

The federal government had no authority to grant or take away state Citizenship because the people formed the governments and were bound by duty and fealty to the state (freely committed by the people), and those states were sovereign in determining who their People/Citizens were. Remember that states are a Body of People that are individually part of a Republic. Hence the term, "Self-Governed."

The Tenth Amendment makes the distinction clear: **"The powers not delegated to the United States by the Constitution, nor prohibited by it to the States, are reserved to the States respectively, or to the people."**

This **reinforces** the fact that the **United States is an entity that only possesses limited, delegated powers**, while the states and the people retain sovereignty. Conversely, as we'll expand on later, the **Supremacy Clause ensures that states cannot make laws that directly violate the Federal Constitution.**

State Citizenship and Popular Sovereignty (1789-1857)

Highlighting State Citizens in Early Jurisprudence

The early Supreme Court consistently distinguished between state and federal jurisdictions. State Citizens were seen as the republic's foundation, with their rights protected primarily by their states.

Sovereignty Resides in the People

The People are endowed by their Creator (the true Sovereign) with certain unalienable rights. This foundational truth was affirmed in *Chisholm v. Georgia* (1793), in which Chief Justice John Jay delivered the majority ruling for the Supreme Court, recognizing that sovereignty resides not in the state itself, but in the People who compose it. The justices declared that the states were not independent sovereigns in their own right, but rather administrative bodies that derive their power from the consent of the governed. The Declaration of Independence affirms that governments exist solely to secure the rights of the People, and when they fail in this duty, their legitimacy is called into question.

"At the Revolution, the sovereignty devolved on the people; and they are truly the sovereigns of the country—but they are *sovereigns without subjects* (unless the African slaves among us may be so called)—and have none to govern but *themselves*—the citizens of America are equal as fellow citizens, and as joint tenants in the sovereignty." - Justice John Jay.

The Eleventh Amendment, state Citizenship, and Sovereignty of the People

One of the most persistent myths is the notion that the Eleventh (11th) Amendment (1795) overturned *Chisholm v. Georgia,* and in doing so, somehow displaced the foundational principle that the People are the true sovereigns. This falsehood has led many to believe that the states exist as independent, sovereign entities in their own right, rather than as governing bodies that derive all legitimate authority from the People. However, the 11th Amendment did not and could not alter the fundamental truth recognized in *Chisholm*: that sovereignty resides with the People, whom have merely delegated certain powers to the states and federal government.

"The Judicial power of the United States shall not be construed to extend to any suit in law or equity, commenced or prosecuted against one of the

United States by Citizens of another State, or by Citizens or Subjects of any Foreign State."

The 11th Amendment simply says that states could not be sued in federal court by citizens of other states. The amendment also applies to federal suits against states brought by private parties, regardless of citizenship, without their consent. So then, did the 11th Amendment grant sovereignty? Or did it strip the People of their supreme authority? Neither, as the states do not exist outside the will of the People, nor does the 11th Amendment grant them some newfound, absolute power.

The false belief that the 11th Amendment fundamentally altered the sovereignty of the People has caused many to lose faith in their standing as Citizens, but the truth remains unchanged: neither Congress nor the states, nor any constitutional amendment, can undo the self-evident fact that the People are the ultimate sovereigns. To claim otherwise is to reject the very premise upon which the nation was founded…that governments derive their just powers from the consent of the governed.

Reconciling *Chisholm v. Georgia* and the 11th Amendment

The ruling in *Chisholm* reaffirmed a fundamental truth: **sovereignty resides with the People, not the states**. The Court held that a state *could* be sued in federal court by a Citizen of another state, reasoning that since the People ratified the Constitution, the states were subject to the judicial authority granted by Article III. In response, the 11th Amendment was quickly ratified, restricting federal jurisdiction by prohibiting private Citizens from suing a state in federal court without its consent.

Despite this restriction, the 11th Amendment did not overturn the principle that the People are the true sovereigns; rather, it clarified the limits of federal judicial power over the states. In *Barron v. Baltimore*, 32 U.S. 243 (1833), the Supreme Court, under Chief Justice John Marshall, ruled on the limitation of federal power. In *Barron*, the court made it clear that the Bill of Rights did not restrain state governments, meaning state citizens had to rely on their own state constitutions for the protection of their rights. The states, while subordinate to the People, retain a level of sovereignty as parties to the constitutional compact; however, the 11th Amendment restricts access to federal courts, and states remain accountable through their own courts, through the Supreme Court in cases between states, and in cases where Congress may abrogate immunity. Thus, while the 11th Amendment reshaped the procedural landscape, it did not, and could not, displace the foundational principle that all government authority is derived from the People.

Relevant Supreme Court Case References

- **Chisholm v. Georgia, 2 U.S. 419 (1793):** The Court recognized the sovereignty of the states and the role of Citizens as the ultimate sovereigns.

- **Calder v. Bull, 3 U.S. 386 (1798):** Affirmed the importance of natural law and the social contract, emphasizing the rights of individuals within the framework of state sovereignty.

- **Gibbons v. Ogden, 22 U.S. 1 (1824):** Clarified the powers reserved to the states versus those delegated to the federal government.

- **Barron v. Baltimore, 32 U.S. 243 (1833):** The Supreme Court held that the Bill of Rights restricts only the powers of the federal government and do not apply to state governments.

- **Dred Scott v. Sandford, 60 U.S. 393 (1857):** The Court declared: "The Citizens of the United States at the time of the adoption of the Constitution were Citizens of the several states." This case highlighted the distinction between state Citizens and any evolving notion of federal citizenship.

State of the Union
Citizenship vs. U.S. Citizenship

CHAPTER 2

The Creation of Federal Citizenship (U.S. citizen) (1865-1870)

Introduction

The Thirteenth (13th), Fourteenth (14th), and Fifteenth (15th) Amendments, also known as the Reconstruction Amendments, were passed after the Civil War. These Amendments fundamentally altered the relationship between the federal government, the states, and individual citizens. While the 13th Amendment abolished slavery and involuntary servitude, the 14th Amendment notably created a federal (U.S.) citizen, and the 15th Amendment guaranteed voting rights for citizens of the United States. It also marked a significant departure from earlier constitutional principles regarding state sovereignty and federal jurisdiction. This section will focus on the 14th Amendment as it relates to citizenship and how it does (or does not) affect state Citizenship and sovereignty.

State Citizens vs. Federal Citizens of the United States under the 14th Amendment

Before the 14th Amendment (1868), the Federal Constitution restricted the federal government, not the states. Though *Barron* restricted the Bill of Rights to the federal government in application, the Supremacy Clause

(Article VI, Clause 2) ensures that states could not override federally protected rights either.

While redress has been narrowed by judicial interpretations, especially regarding the 11th Amendment and state immunity, avenues still exist for the People to hold their state governments accountable. Let's not forget that the fundamental principle remains unchanged: governments exist only with the consent of the governed, and the People remain the sovereigns.

Supremacy Clause: *"This Constitution, and the Laws of the United States which shall be made in Pursuance thereof; and all Treaties made, or which shall be made, under the Authority of the United States, shall be the supreme Law of the Land; and the Judges in every State shall be bound thereby, any Thing in the Constitution or Laws of any State to the Contrary notwithstanding."*

The 14th Amendment - Citizenship Clause

With the so-called/questionable ratification of the 14th Amendment, a fundamental shift occurred in the original constitutional framework. This amendment introduced a federal definition of citizenship, effectively creating a new class of citizens distinct from the original state Citizens.

A prevailing misconception is that the 14th Amendment abolished state Citizenship or that state rights became secondary to the rights granted by the federal Constitution. However, this is not the case. It is important to remember that the People were never parties to the federal Constitution or its Bill of Rights, as discussed previously. To fully understand this transformation, let us analyze the text of the Citizenship Clause (14th Amendment, Section 1):

"All persons born or naturalized in the United States, and subject to the jurisdiction thereof, are citizens of the United States and of the State wherein they reside."

Here, the 14th Amendment creates a distinction between:

1. A citizen of a State.

2. "Citizens of the United States", a new federal class of citizenship for "persons" subject to the jurisdiction of the federal government. (Employees of a Company)

The Legal Distinctions in the 14th Amendment's Language

- The term "persons" in legal usage often refers to an artificial legal entity, distinct from a living man or woman. This terminology suggests that 14th Amendment citizens are persons and subjects of the U.S. government, rather than state Citizens ("We the People" aka the sovereigns).

- The phrase "and subject to the jurisdiction thereof" is a crucial qualifier. It implies a presumption, that being born in the United States automatically places one under federal jurisdiction. However, this is not an absolute rule; it does not mean that mere birth on U.S. soil automatically confers U.S. citizenship; jurisdiction must be established, not assumed. Full political jurisdiction excludes certain groups, such as foreign diplomats' children and members of sovereign Native tribes (before 1924).

Note: The 14th Amendment was enacted primarily to grant citizenship to formerly enslaved individuals, overturning *Dred Scott v. Sandford* (1857), which had wrongly denied "negros" and "blacks" U.S. citizenship. However, this new federal citizenship was separate from state Citizenship, which preexisted and remained distinct. State Citizens had unalienable rights under their state constitutions, whereas U.S. citizens were now recognized under federal law. **The 14th Amendment did not abolish state Citizenship, it merely created a new class of federal citizen subject to a different jurisdiction.** To clarify, there are two types of jurisdiction at play here:

- o **Territorial jurisdiction** is less about geography and more about contractual nexus. When one identifies as residing within a STATE (corporate entity) and uses a ZIP CODE (a federal postal zone), they are presumed to have entered into a jurisdictional contract. Thus, presence alone isn't what binds…it's the **legal fiction of domicile, consent, and participation in federal territories and programs** that creates enforceable obligations under statutory law.

- o Political jurisdiction – The condition of being subject to the full legal and political authority of the United States government through allegiance.

- The use of "citizens" (lowercase) rather than "Citizens" (uppercase) is significant. In legal contexts, a proper noun typically refers to a specific sovereign body, while a common noun can denote a more general or subordinate status.

- The term "reside" (as in "State wherein they reside") is also legally significant. In modern jurisprudence, "residence" (or "resident") is a legal designation that differs from the lawful term's "inhabitant" or "domicile".

  o A resident is someone who lives in a place temporarily or for legal purposes.

  o An inhabitant is someone who has a permanent, fixed presence in a given place.

  o This distinction matters because 14th Amendment citizenship ties state citizenship to mere residence, whereas prior to the 14th Amendment, a state Citizen could live in another state without losing their original state Citizenship.

  Note: A state Citizen's nationality was tied to their allegiance to a State, not to the United States. Example: A person born in New York was a New Yorker by nationality. If they moved and inhabited another state, let's say Maryland, they did not automatically become a "Marylander" unless they formally changed their allegiance.

The federal government lacked the authority to grant or revoke state Citizenship because states were the sole arbiters of who their Citizens were. State Citizens have unalienable rights that are beyond federal interference. The new U.S. citizen, however, is only granted privileges and immunities, not inherent, God-given, unalienable rights.

In summary, the 14th Amendment is a double-edged sword which shields natural rights from state abuse, but also forges a new class of federal "citizen" subject to expansive statutory control. Most people today are **unwittingly presumed to be 14th Amendment citizens** through implied consent to a legal identity, namely, the birth certificate and its derivative instruments (associated federal benefits). As a **state Citizen**, you stand in your unalienable authority, endowed by the Sovereign Creator, owing allegiance to your state; not to federal jurisdiction. The remedy is to **withdraw your consent** and remain outside the federal construct and statutory reach.

Relevant Case References

- **Slaughter-House Cases, 83 U.S. 36 (1873):** the Supreme Court distinguished between state Citizenship and newly created federal Citizenship: "It is quite clear, then, that there is a citizenship of the United States, and a citizenship of a State, which are distinct from each other..." Majority Opinion by Justice Samuel F. Miller

- **United States v. Cruikshank, 92 U.S. 542 (1875):** Reaffirmed the limited scope of federal power, emphasizing states' rights even under the 14th Amendment. The Court stated:

  o "The rights of Citizens are derived primarily from the state, and not from the United States."

  o "The phrase 'Citizen of the United States' and 'Citizens of a State' are distinct from each other, and depend upon different characteristics or circumstances in the individual." Majority Opinion by Chief Justice Morrison R. Waite.

CHAPTER 3

————— ❧❧ —————

The Gradual Federalization
of Citizenship (1870–1970)

Over time, Congress has expanded the application of U.S. citizenship, often at the expense of the uninformed populus, but not without interpretation from the courts, making the government's intent ever so clear to create a subclass of citizens. A prevalent theme in the Reconstruction Amendments was the enforcement provisions (final clause) which granted Congress broad authority to set a precedent for increased federal oversight over individual rights and state affairs.

The clause, "Congress shall have power to enforce this article by appropriate legislation", is a significant departure from earlier constitutional principles regarding state sovereignty and federal jurisdiction. This enforcement provision gave Congress broad authority to pass laws for increased federal oversight over individual rights and state affairs.

The Organic Act of 1871

In 1871, The Organic Act marked a turning point in American history, marking a departure from the original framework of America as a Republic. The act fundamentally altered the structure of the federal government by forming the District of Columbia into a municipal corporation under direct congressional control. By consolidating authority within the District of Columbia as a corporate entity, Congress established a mechanism to undermine popular and state sovereignty.

The corporatization of the federal government under the Organic Act was reinforced through subsequent acts of usurpation, each contributing to the shift from the Republic's original framework:

- **1933 – Public Law 73-10 (HJR 192), 48 Stat. 112**: The federal government abandoned the gold standard, nullifying Citizens' ability to settle debts in real money and replacing it with a system of debt-based currency controlled by private banking interests. This move fundamentally altered economic sovereignty, making all financial transactions subject to federal regulation.

- **1935 – Social Security Act, 49 Stat. 620, codified at 42 U.S.C. § 301 et seq.**: This Act formalized federal dependency by establishing a nationwide identification and benefit system, linking individuals to the federal government rather than their state of birth. In doing so, it replaced state Citizenship with a federal welfare structure, further diminishing personal sovereignty.

- **1940 – The Buck Act, 4 U.S.C. §§ 105–110**: This Act allowed the federal government to extend its jurisdiction over state governments by treating federal territories and areas within states (such as federal enclaves) as part of federal jurisdiction. This created legal confusion regarding the distinction between state sovereignty and federal oversight.

- **1946 – Administrative Procedure Act, 60 Stat. 237, codified at 5 U.S.C. § 551 et seq.**: This Act solidified the power of federal agencies, effectively bypassing constitutional checks and subjecting all Citizens to administrative rule rather than common law or state protections. It marked the expansion of the bureaucratic state, removing judicial recourse and placing governance into the hands of unelected officials. By establishing a federal framework for administrative agencies, this Act influenced how states implemented bureaucratic governance, leading to a shift from a government of laws to a government of regulatory agencies.

- **1952 – Uniform Commercial Code, first published in 1952 by the National Conference of Commissioners on Uniform State Laws and the American Law Institute**: The UCC effectively restructured how state governments operated by shifting governance from a constitutional framework to a commercial framework. States adopted the UCC as a means of streamlining commerce, but in doing so, they incorporated themselves into the larger corporate structure dictated by federal and international financial systems.

- **Present – State Incorporation under Dun & Bradstreet**: Many states and municipalities registered as corporate entities within a business directory, effectively functioning as corporate franchises of the larger federal system.

Federal courts reinforced this consolidation of power, using the 14th Amendment as a legal tool to justify federal dominance:

- **1880 – Ex parte Virginia**: This ruling expanded federal enforcement powers under the 14th Amendment, overriding state jurisdiction in legal matters that were once exclusively under the states' domain.

- **1908 – Twining v. New Jersey**: This case began the selective incorporation of federal laws against the states, diminishing state sovereignty and eroding the distinction between state and federal jurisdiction.

- **1938 – Court Rulings Such as Erie Railroad Co. v. Tompkins**: This case eliminated the distinction between general federal common law and state common law, effectively forcing states through incorporation, to comply with federal legal standards that prioritized commercial interests.

- **1967 – Afroyim v. Rusk**: In this ruling, the Supreme Court elevated U.S. citizenship above state Citizenship, effectively nullifying any legal distinction between the two and eliminating the independent status of state Citizens.

Relevant Case References

- **Ex parte Virginia, 100 U.S. 339 (1880):** Expanded federal enforcement powers under the 14th Amendment.

- **Twining v. New Jersey, 211 U.S. 78 (1908):** Began the process of incorporating federal rights.

- **Court Rulings, Such as Erie Railroad Co. v. Tompkins (1938):** Eliminated the distinction between general federal common law and state common law.

- **Afroyim v. Rusk, 387 U.S. 253 (1967):** The Supreme Court held that U.S. citizenship cannot be involuntarily revoked by the government, affirming the constitutional protection of federal citizenship under the Fourteenth Amendment. It also held that once acquired, citizenship is not a mere privilege granted by Congress, but a protected political status <u>that may only be relinquished by voluntary act of the individual.</u>

CHAPTER 4

State Citizenship Today
(1970 - Present)

The Republic Still Exists Under God and Constitutional Law

The undeniable fact that two governments exist in America is made clear by U.S. Supreme Court Justice Marshall Harlan in his dissenting opinion in Downes v. Bidwell, 182 U.S. 244, (1901). Justice Harlan said,

"The idea prevails...with some indeed, it found expression in arguments at the bar that we have in this country substantially or practically two national governments; one to be maintained under the Constitution [de jure], with all its restrictions; the other to be maintained by Congress [de facto], outside and independently of that instrument by exercising such powers as other nations of the earth are accustomed to exercise."

The Guarantee Clause in Article IV, Section 4 ensures that every state retains a Republican form of government, preventing the federal government from lawfully altering this structure. In **Luther v. Borden, 48 U.S. 1 (1849),** the Supreme Court held that the Republican form of government cannot be arbitrarily replaced by democratic rule, underscoring the fixed rights inherent in a Republic.

While the corporate nature of the federal government may obscure this reality, the Republic remains intact. This ensures that neither legislative nor administrative action can lawfully deprive the People of their fundamental liberties. Remember that *Chisholm* affirmed the people (state Citizens) were the sovereigns, and that holding has never been overturned. Despite modern governance operating under a corporate framework, the lawful Republic still exists, waiting for informed Citizens to reassert their rightful place under constitutional law.

Revoking Contracts and Withdrawing from the U.S. Corporate System

Article I, Section 10, Clause 1:

> "No State shall enter into any Treaty, Alliance, or Confederation; grant Letters of Marque and Reprisal; coin Money; emit Bills of Credit; make any Thing but gold and silver Coin a Tender in Payment of Debts; pass any Bill of Attainder, ex post facto Law, or Law impairing the Obligation of Contracts, or grant any Title of Nobility."

At the heart of lawful governance is the principle that contracts dictate the law. The Contract Clause (Article I, Section 10, Clause 1) of the Constitution explicitly states that no state shall pass any law impairing the obligation of contracts. **This is the essence of self-governance**. This affirms that lawful agreements, not government mandates, determine your status. Under common law and admiralty principles, jurisdiction is established through consent, and contracts serve as the primary mechanism through which people become subjects. The same clause also explicitly prohibits states from passing any "Bill of Attainder, ex post facto Law, or Law impairing the Obligation of Contracts," which underscores the inviolability of lawful agreements, ensuring that once a contract is made, its terms cannot be retroactively altered or nullified by state legislation. This protection is foundational to the Republic, emphasizing that contracts dictate the law.

Allegiance

Allegiance is the foundation of Citizenship because it defines one's political and legal obligations. A state Citizen owes allegiance to their state and the People who comprise it, maintaining sovereignty under a Republican form of government, while a U.S. citizen pledges allegiance to the United States (corporation) and has duties, debts, and obligations. A U.S. citizen is bound by statutory obligations due to adhesion contracts; agreements that grant personal, territorial and political jurisdiction to the United States corporation and its state (STATE) franchises. Examples of these adhesion contracts include, but are not limited to, the following:

- Birth Certificates (Foundational Identity Document with Implied Social Contract)

- Passports

- Voter Registration

- W-4, W-2 Employment Agreements

- Social Security Enrollment

- Driver's Licenses

- Marriage Licenses

- Gun Registration, and the like

<u>By rescinding these contracts and pledging allegiance solely to their state</u> <u>(which is the People), individuals can lawfully remove themselves from</u> <u>the federal corporate structure and reclaim the Republic.</u> This principle was reaffirmed in Bond v. United States, 564 U.S. 211 (2011). It demonstrated that **individuals possess personal sovereignty** and are entitled to challenge unlawful exercises of federal power. The People are the law, and by rejecting imposed contracts, they reaffirm their sovereign standing under God, free from external control.

The Misconception of "Sovereign Citizens"

It's critical to understand the difference between the sovereign citizen movement and the concept of state Citizenship. The term "sovereign citizen," which is inherently contradictory, has emerged to describe individuals who claim personal sovereignty while often rejecting governmental authority. However, many who adopt this label do so unwittingly, failing to recognize the critical distinction between a U.S. citizen who, through contractual obligations, owes allegiance to the federal corporate entity, and a Citizen of a state of the Union, who is a true sovereign within the Republic.

State Citizen is NOT a concept. State Citizenship is grounded both in our Supreme Courts and constitutional principles and deeply rooted in America's history and framework. The concept of "sovereign citizen" is a misnomer that often leads people to take unsound legal positions, such as making meritless claims because they cannot provide any proof to refute or rebut the jurisdiction to which they are bound to by contract. By recognizing the importance of contracts and the distinction between state and federal jurisdictions, the People can reassert their rightful place as the sovereigns of the Republic.

The conflation of terms like "sovereign citizen" and "Democratic Republic" serves to mislead the populace. A Republic is based on God-given unalienable rights and common law principles, whereas a Democracy operates on majority rule, which can potentially infringe upon individual liberties. This deliberate misrepresentation diverts attention from the People's true standing and power within the Republic. The Declaration of Independence (1776) remains a testament to the People's right to alter or abolish any government that violates their natural rights. By understanding and embracing the principles of state Citizenship, individuals can reclaim their sovereignty and restore the Republic to its foundational ideals.

The concept of sovereignty has been deliberately misrepresented to discredit the People and undermine the foundation of the Republic. The term "sovereign citizen", a phrase with no legal definition, has been strategically employed by corporate and governmental institutions to label dissenters as domestic threats. This mischaracterization serves a dual purpose:

1. To delegitimize lawful challenges to corporate governmental overreach, and

2. To obscure the fact that the true Republic still exists and remains accessible through state Citizenship grounded in allegiance, not federal benefit.

True sovereignty is not about rejecting lawful governance, but about understanding jurisdiction, and most importantly, how that jurisdiction is contractually invoked. It is not defiance that binds individuals to object federal control; it is contractual entanglement while other silent agreements are entered into knowingly or unknowingly.

The solution lies in rescinding these contracts, correcting status, and reestablishing allegiance to one's sovereign state under natural and common law. This is the peaceful and lawful path to restoring individual sovereignty and the original constitutional Republic.

The Misconception of the terms "national", "national of the United States", and "state National"

Definitions

1. National: A "national" is a person who owes permanent allegiance to a state. 8 U.S.C. § 1101(a)(21)

2. American National: A made up term with no grounding in law or code.

3. National of the United States (US national): A citizen of the United States, or a person who, though not a citizen of the United States, owes permanent allegiance to the United States. 8 U.S.C. § 1101(a)(22).

4. State National: Another made up term with no grounding in law or code. The term "State National" does not have a definition in the United States Code. Neither does it have a definition in any other official federal statutes, nor the Immigration and Nationality Act. It is often used by individuals associated with the "sovereign citizen" movement to describe a person who claims to be a national of a specific U.S. state and not subject to federal laws.

5. Non-citizen National: means a person who owes permanent allegiance to the United States, as distinguished from allegiance to a foreign state, and who has not acquired U.S. citizenship under Title III of the Immigration and Nationality Act or other applicable law or treaty." 22 CFR § 51.1

- Also defined: **"U.S. national"** includes both U.S. citizens and non-citizen nationals.

These subclass citizenships, which are all codified and made up, serve the administrative framework of the federal corporation known as the United States which actually redirects allegiance to federal authority. The 14th Amendment introduced a distinct class of federal citizenship, marked by the use of the lowercase "citizen," reflecting a shift in legal status from sovereign allegiance to federal jurisdiction. This change redefined citizenship not as a matter of state allegiance and natural rights but as a political status subject to federal authority. Similarly, the term "state" as defined in certain federal statutes (e.g., 8 U.S.C. § 1101(a)(36)) explicitly includes federal territories and possessions, which does not refer to the sovereign States of the Union as recognized at the founding.

These distinctions are not arbitrary, they are crucial. Contracts, statutes, and legal definitions hinge on terminology. Most Americans are unaware of the legal consequences of terms like "person," "resident," or "individual," which are often used to imply jurisdiction and consent. For example, while 8 U.S.C. § 1101(a)(21) defines a "national" as someone who owes permanent allegiance to a "state," that "state" is legally defined to include federal territories. Despite sounding benign, such definitions establish contractual jurisdiction with the federal government; not with the states of the Union.

Supreme Court precedents overwhelmingly affirm the legitimacy and distinct legal status of state Citizenship, yet provide no statutory or judicial support for terms such as "state national" or "American national." These latter terms, often promoted by individuals unfamiliar with established law, lack foundation in the U.S. Code or recognized case law. As a result, their use is frequently viewed by courts and government entities as frivolous or misleading, and has led many to be improperly associated with the so-called "sovereign citizen" label, a term that itself has no legal definition but is often used pejoratively to marginalize lawful dissent.

The key to reclaiming state Citizenship lies in understanding these legal distinctions and removing oneself from contracts and designations that invoke federal authority. That begins with informed language, lawful documentation, and a clear understanding of one's standing under the original constitutional compact.

Relevant Case References

- **Downes v. Bidwell, 182 U.S. 244 (1901)** – Recognized a dual system of government: one "de jure" under the Constitution and a second "de facto" exercised by Congress over unincorporated territories.

- **Bond v. United States, 564 U.S. 211 (2011)** –Affirmed that an individual can challenge federal overreach under the Tenth (10th) Amendment.

- **Article I, Section 10, Clause 1** - Contract Clause of the Constitution

- **Luther v. Borden, 48 U.S. 1 (1849)** - Held that the Republican form of government cannot be arbitrarily replaced by democratic rule.

- **The Declaration of Independence (1776)** - Remains a legal foundation affirming that People have the right to alter or abolish a government that violates their natural rights.

- **The Guarantee Clause (Article IV, Section 4)** - Ensures that every state maintains a Republican form of government. The federal government cannot lawfully alter this structure, despite operating as a corporate entity.

- **Afroyim v. Rusk, 387 U.S. 253 (1967)** - Recognized that Citizenship is a matter of allegiance and cannot be taken away involuntarily.

CHAPTER 5

The Two Systems Explained: Quick Recap

1. The Original Political Compact: The United States of America

- Founded under **the Declaration of Independence (1776)** and **Articles of Confederation (1781)**

- Sovereign states formed a confederation, each with its own citizens and internal laws.

- State citizenship meant allegiance to a state, with protections under Article IV, Section 2 of the Constitution:
  "The Citizens of each State shall be entitled to all Privileges and Immunities of Citizens in the several States."

- This was the only recognized form of national allegiance until post-Civil War.

2. The Corporate Entity: The United States (Federal Jurisdiction)

- The **14th Amendment (1868)** created a **new class of citizenship**:
  "All persons born or naturalized in the United States... are citizens of the United States and of the State wherein they reside."

- This "United States" is **not** the organic union of sovereign states; it is a **federal corporate overlay** (see: *United States v. Cruikshank, 92 U.S. 542*).

LEGAL RECOGNITION OF THE DUAL SYSTEM

Here is how the cases reinforce the divide:

U.S. Citizenship (Federal Jurisdiction)

- **Slaughterhouse Cases (1873)**: "There is a distinction between the privileges of state citizens and citizens of the United States."

- **United States v. Anthony (1873)**: "A United States citizen is a special class created by Congress."

- **Belmont v. Gulfport (1929)**: "Electors [state Citizens] are not taxpayers."

- **Jones v. Temmer (1993)**: The 14th Amendment protects *very few* rights; mostly those tied to federal citizenship.

- **Bond v. United States (2000)**: The Federal government's power is limited unless consented to via citizenship and jurisdiction.

State Citizenship (Organic, Common Law Jurisdiction)

- **Paul v. Virginia (1868)**: Rights are tied to state citizenship, not transferable across states without consent.

- **Colgate v. Harvey (1935)**: Federal and state governments are distinct; so are their citizens. Although the case was overruled in 1940, the distinction between the Federal and state governments remains intact.

- **Crosse v. Board of Supervisors (1966)**: No requirement exists for a state citizen to be a U.S. citizen. Both before and after the Fourteenth Amendment to the federal Constitution, it has not been necessary for a person to be a citizen of the United States in order to be a citizen of his state.

- **Gardina v. Board of Registrars (1909)**: "Two classes of citizens: one of the United States and one of the State." The decision analyzes the distinction between state and federal citizenship, explaining the constitutional provisions governing who is considered a citizen capable of voting.

- **State v. Fowler (1889)**: "A person may be a state citizen but not a U.S. citizen." In explaining its view, the court distinguished "citizen of a State" from "citizen of the United States." The opinion acknowledged that the labels are not identical and are distinct concepts of citizenship.

- **Downes v. Bidwell 182 U.S. 244 (1901):** Dissenting opinion by Justice Marshall Harlan: *The idea prevails with some-- indeed, it found expression in arguments at the bar—that we have in this country substantially or practically two national governments; one to be maintained under the Constitution [de jure], with all its restrictions; the other to be maintained by Congress [de facto], outside and independently of that* *instrument by exercising such powers as other nations of the earth are accustomed to exercise."*

THE TRAP: "Choice Without Knowledge"

Here's how the confusion was orchestrated:

- The 14th Amendment created a **default federal citizenship**.

- Federal benefits (SSNs, passports, licenses) required identifying as a **U.S. citizen**, without disclosing that **this was a contractual status**.

- State citizenship became **presumed abandoned** unless **affirmatively claimed**.

- Administrative law and statutory presumption (e.g. IRS, DMV) presume U.S. citizenship and its obligations unless rebutted.

THE PATH TO FREEDOM UNDER THE DECLARATION

You still have the lawful **right to choose allegiance** to your **state republic** under:

- **The Declaration of Independence (1776)**

- **Article IV, Section 2** – privileges and immunities of **Citizens of the several States**

- **Cases recognizing your right to be a state citizen without being a federal one:**
  - *State v. Fowler*

- *McDonel v. The State*
- *U.S. v. Cruikshank*
- *Crosse v. Board of Supervisors*

NEXT STEPS FOR ASSERTING YOUR CHOICE

1. **Establish your state citizenship** on record; domicile, intent, declarations, and lawful processes.

2. **Rebut the presumption of U.S. citizenship**; through affidavits, passport processes, and withdrawal of consent.

3. **Document your lawful status** with clarity, consistency, and knowledge.

4. **Join HISAdvocates.org**

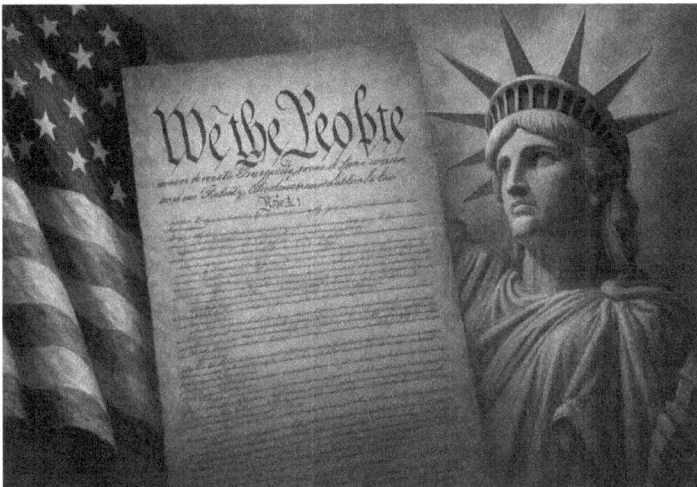

CHAPTER 6

The Choice is Yours:
Reclaim Your Freedom

Reclaiming your state Citizenship and restoring the Republic is not just a process, it's a return to your unalienable rights, your natural sovereignty, and your rightful place under the laws of nature and the Constitution. For generations, Americans have operated within a restructured system that redefined their status and gradually eroded the liberties endowed by their Creator.

Yet knowledge restores agency. As Thomas Jefferson warned, "The natural progress of things is for liberty to yield, and government to gain ground." This truth confronts us today. The Republic can be revived only when the People reclaim their rightful status and reestablish lawful self-governance.

James Madison wrote, "The advancement and diffusion of knowledge is the only guardian of true liberty." That is why our mission at HIS Advocates is to educate, equip, and support those ready to take meaningful action. Once you grasp the true nature of your unalienable rights, continued submission to administrative control becomes untenable.

Now, the choice is yours.

☑ **Call:** Are You Ready to Become Free Now? Call us today at **(844) 447-2386 (HIS Advo)** Option 2 to start your journey.

☑ **Join:** For more information about HISAdvocates.org, sign up for our free membership using this link https://www.hisadvocates.org/join.

☑ **Download:** Visit us on your computer at HISAdvocates.TV to join our official channel, use this link https://hisadvocates.tv/login or download our App from your smartphone. Search "HISAdvocates.TV" on your Android or iPhone store.

☑ **Book Now:** Have Questions? Book a Live appointment with one of our team members to get answers to your questions. **Click Here to Book Now: HISFreedom.org**

☑ **Upgrade:** Want to Go Deeper? Upgrade your **HIS Advocates Membership to VIP** and gain exclusive access to resources, expert guidance, and a community committed to true freedom. **Click Here to Upgrade: HISVIP.org**

The time for waiting is over. The time for action is now. The Republic needs its People to rise…**will you answer the call?**

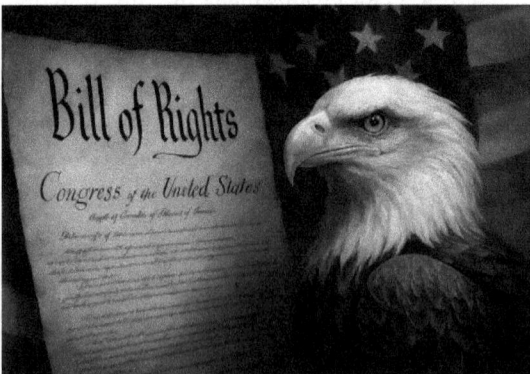

Authoritative and Case Law

The 14th Amendment

The Citizenship Clause states: "All persons born or naturalized in the United States, and subject to the jurisdiction thereof, are citizens of the United States and of the State wherein they reside." This marked a shift from the original framework, creating a federal definition of citizenship that subordinated state Citizenship.

Full Text of the 14th Amendment:

Section 1. All persons born or naturalized in the United States, and subject to the jurisdiction thereof, are citizens of the United States and of the State wherein they reside. No State shall make or enforce any law which shall abridge the privileges or immunities of citizens of the United States; nor shall any State deprive any person of life, liberty, or property, without due process of law; nor deny to any person within its jurisdiction the equal protection of the laws.

Section 2. Representatives shall be apportioned among the several States according to their respective numbers, counting the whole number of persons in each State, excluding Indians not taxed. But when the right to vote at any election for the choice of electors for President and Vice President of the United States, Representatives in Congress, the Executive and Judicial officers of a State, or the members of the

Legislature thereof, is denied to any of the male inhabitants of such State, being twenty-one years of age, and citizens of the United States, or in any way abridged, except for participation in rebellion, or other crime, the basis of representation therein shall be reduced in the proportion which the number of such male citizens shall bear to the whole number of male citizens twenty-one years of age in such State.

Section 3. No person shall be a Senator or Representative in Congress, or elector of President and Vice President, or hold any office, civil or military, under the United States, or under any State, who, having previously taken an oath, as a member of Congress, or as an officer of the United States, or as a member of any State legislature, or as an executive or judicial officer of any State, to support the Constitution of the United States, shall have engaged in insurrection or rebellion against the same, or given aid or comfort to the enemies thereof. But Congress may by a vote of two-thirds of each House, remove such disability.

Section 4. The validity of the public debt of the United States, authorized by law, including debts incurred for payment of pensions and bounties for services in suppressing insurrection or rebellion, shall not be questioned. But neither the United States nor any State shall assume or pay any debt or obligation incurred in aid of insurrection or rebellion against the United States, or any claim for the loss or emancipation of any slave; but all such debts, obligations, and claims shall be held illegal and void.

Section 5. The Congress shall have the power to enforce, by appropriate legislation, the provisions of this article.

Selected Quotes and Excerpts from Court Cases

Slaughter-House Cases: "It is quite clear, then, that there is a citizenship of the United States, and a citizenship of a State, which are distinct from each other."

United States v. Cruikshank: "The government of the United States is one of delegated, limited, and enumerated powers."

State Constitutions and Legal Codes:

- **California Constitution, Article I:** Guarantees individual freedoms and the sovereignty of the state government.

- **Texas Constitution, Article IV:** Establishes the rights and privileges of state Citizens and affirms state independence within the federal system.

Slaughter-House Cases, 83 U.S. 36 (1873)

"It is quite clear, then, that there is a citizenship of the United States, and a citizenship of a State, which are distinct from each other."

United States v. Cruikshank, 92 U.S. 542 (1875)

"The government of the United States is one of delegated, limited, and enumerated powers."

Dred Scott v. Sandford, 60 U.S. 393 (1857)

"The Citizens of the United States at the time of the adoption of the Constitution were Citizens of the several states."

References to State Constitutions and Legal Codes

California Constitution, Article I

"All people are by nature free and independent and have inalienable rights. Among these are enjoying and defending life and liberty, acquiring, possessing, and protecting property, and pursuing and obtaining safety, happiness, and privacy."

Texas Constitution, Article IV

"The faith of the State of Texas shall remain pledged to the preservation of a republican form of government, and to the sovereignty of the State and its protection from any encroachment by the federal government."

New York Civil Rights Law, Section 4

"The right of the people to assemble and consult for the common good, and to petition the government or any department thereof, shall never be abridged."

Case Citations and Legal References

Case Citations

- **Afroyim v. Rusk, 387 U.S. 253 (1967):** Affirmed the principle that U.S. citizenship cannot be involuntarily revoked. This decision reinforced the sanctity of citizenship, ensuring that individuals cannot be stripped of their U.S. citizenship without their consent, even in cases of expatriation or acts perceived as renouncing allegiance. It emphasized the constitutional protection of individual rights under the Fourteenth Amendment and solidified the view that citizenship is a fundamental right, safeguarded from arbitrary governmental action.

- **Barron v. Baltimore, 32 U.S. 243 (1833):** Defined the limitations of the Bill of Rights on federal vs. state governments.

- **Calder v. Bull, 3 U.S. 386 (1798):** Emphasized the role of natural law in legal interpretation.

- **Chisholm v. Georgia, 2 U.S. 419 (1793):** Highlighted state sovereignty under the Constitution.

- **Downes v. Bidwell, 182 U.S. 244 (1901)** – Recognized a dual system of government: one "de jure" under the Constitution and a second "de facto" exercised by Congress over unincorporated territories.

- **Dred Scott v. Sandford, 60 U.S. 393 (1857):** Differentiated state Citizenship from federal citizenship.

- **Ex parte Virginia, 100 U.S. 339 (1880):** Addressed federal enforcement powers under the 14th Amendment.

- **Gibbons v. Ogden, 22 U.S. 1 (1824):** Clarified state vs. federal powers regarding interstate commerce.

- **Slaughter-House Cases, 83 U.S. 36 (1873):** Distinguished between state and federal citizenship.

- **Twining v. New Jersey, 211 U.S. 78 (1908):** Began incorporation of federal rights against state actions.

- **United States v. Cruikshank, 92 U.S. 542 (1875):** U.S. citizenship cannot be involuntarily revoked by the government; but a protected political status that may only be relinquished by voluntary act of the individual.

Disclaimer: The cases below are the major reversals among the cases listed above, and exactly what element was reversed:

1. **Chisholm v. Georgia (1793) – Jurisdiction,** not merits, was reversed by the **Eleventh Amendment (1795),** which stripped federal courts of the power to hear "a suit…commenced or prosecuted against one of the United States by Citizens of another State."

   ○ *Element reversed*: The Supreme Court's recognition that *states could be sued in federal court* by private citizens was nullified.

2. **Dred Scott v. Sandford (1857)** – **Substantive holding** that "Africans…were not intended to be included under the word 'citizens'" of the United States was **overturned by the Fourteenth Amendment (1868)**.

   ○ *Element reversed*: The denial of U.S. citizenship to formerly enslaved persons was invalidated by the Amendment's Citizenship Clause.

3. **Barron v. Baltimore (1833)** – Its rule that the Bill of Rights **did not apply to the states** was **effectively reversed** by the **Fourteenth Amendment's Due Process and Equal Protection Clauses**, and subsequent **selective-incorporation decisions** (e.g., *Gitlow v. New York* (1925) for free speech; *Malloy v. Hogan* (1964) for self-incrimination).

   ○ *Element reversed*: The proposition that **no Bill of Rights protection** bound state governments.

4. **Twining v. New Jersey (1908)** – Held that only a *small handful* of privileges & immunities were protected against the states. That narrow reading of the Fourteenth Amendment's Privileges or Immunities Clause was **superseded by selective incorporation doctrine** under the Due Process Clause (e.g., *Palko v. Connecticut* (1937), *McDonald v. Chicago* (2010)).

   ○ *Element reversed*: The limitation on applying most Bill of Rights protections to the states.

Note: The reversals below and interpretive shifts in decisions such as *Chisholm v. Georgia*, *Dred Scott v. Sandford*, *Barron v. Baltimore*, and *Twining v. New Jersey* cannot nullify the fundamental sovereignty of the

People of the several States or the God-given, state-protected rights of their Citizens. Over the centuries, federal power has steadily expanded, often at the expense of the very liberties our Founders sought to preserve because too many have lost sight of their identity as God's creation endowed with natural, unalienable rights and their primary allegiance to HIM, and then as state Citizens. Accepting federal obligations, duties, or debts without this understanding risks granting the federal government broad jurisdictional authority that usurp those inherent rights and strip away the freedoms each state was established to secure.

Statutes and Legal Codes

- **California Constitution, Article I**

- **New York Civil Rights Law, Section 4**

- **Texas Constitution, Article IV**

Federal Constitutional Provisions

- **14th Amendment to the U.S. Constitution**

- **Article IV, Section 2 of the U.S. Constitution**

Key Terms

1. **United States (US)**: Defined in 28 USC § 3002(15)(A) as a *Federal corporation*. Operates primarily in Washington D.C. and federal territories.

2. **United States of America (USA)**: The original confederation of states under the Articles of Confederation and the Constitution. A geographic, lawful union of states.

3. **State Citizen**: A man or woman born or naturalized in one of the 50 states of the Union, retaining allegiance to their state republic, not the federal corporation.

4. **U.S. Citizen**: A legal status created under the 14th Amendment. A person who has accepted corporate benefits, and thereby obligations, of the federal United States.

5. **Legal Person**: An artificial entity created by government (e.g., trust, corporation, corporate citizen).

6. **Natural Man/Woman**: A living being, endowed with unalienable rights, not subject to legislative privileges or contracts unless entered into knowingly and voluntarily.

7. **The People Defined State: state, n.[notice lower case]** "The political system of a **BODY OF PEOPLE** [not bolded or capped in Black's Law Dictionary] who are politically organized; the system of rules by which jurisdiction and authority are exercised

over such a body of people." **Black's Law 11th ed. (an organized body of People)**

8. **The Contracted People: STATE [notice CAPS]** "A STATE is a **COMMUNITY OF PERSONS** [not bolded or capped in Black's Law Dictionary] living within certain limits of territory, under a permanent organization which aims to secure the prevalence of justice by self-imposed law." **Black's Law 11th ed. (people who surrendered their freedom through adhesion contracts/trusts to hold job positions (trustee liable positions) like U.S. citizen, Driver, Voter, Tax Payer, and more)**

9. **Federal State:** "A composite state in which the sovereignty of the entire state is divided between the central or federal government and the local governments of the several constituent states; a union of states in which the control of the external relations of all the member states has been surrendered to a central government so the only state that exists for international purposes is the one formed by the union." **Black's Law 11th ed.**

Appendices

———— ✾ ————

A. **State Citizen vs. U.S. citizen (14th Amendment citizen)
- Tables 1-3**

B. **Territorial Jurisdiction - Table 4**

C. **Federal Union vs. National Government: Key
Distinctions - Tables 5-7**

State Citizen vs. U.S. citizen (14th Amendment citizen)

The tables below highlight the shift from natural, unalienable rights rooted in allegiance to a sovereign state, to statutory privileges tied to residence and benefit participation of a U.S. citizen (14th Amendment citizen). A state Citizen is self-governed under natural law and common law, while a 14th Amendment citizen or "resident" is a legal fiction subject to administrative colorable law. Understanding this distinction is essential to reclaiming one's rightful standing and avoiding involuntary subjection to corporate-state jurisdiction.

Being a "U.S. citizen" is not an identity. It is a role in the corporate structure of the federal government. It's an office, complete with obligations, liabilities, and contracts. Just as one can resign from a corporate job, one can revoke the voluntary contract with the corporate U.S. and return to the private, protected status of a state Citizen under the United States of America. See Bank v. United States, 2000, "A citizen of the United States is a civilly dead entity operating as a co-trustee and co-beneficiary of the public trust...". This understanding restores the lawful order: men and women first, government second. Not the reverse.

Table 1:

Concept	State Citizen	U.S. Citizen
Origin	Constitution / Common Law	14th Amendment / Federal Statute
Jurisdiction	One of the 50 States	District of Columbia / Federal Zones
Entity	Man/Woman	Legal Person / Office Holder
Tax Status	Lawful Non-Taxpayer	Taxpayer by Voluntary Election
Passport	State Citizen with Explanatory Statement	Default U.S. Passport Holder

Table 2:

Concept	Original Understanding	Modern (Statutory) Understanding
Definition of Citizenship	Based on allegiance to a sovereign state and unalienable rights	Based on residence or benefit participation; defined by statute
Rights	Unalienable rights: life, liberty, property, conscience	Privileges granted or regulated by administrative law
Legal Identity	Inhabitant - domiciled by natural right, not under legal compulsion	Resident - legal person subject to statutory jurisdiction
Jurisdiction	Common law and state constitution	Administrative codes, licensing, and regulatory enforcement through contracts

Table 3:

Status	State Citizen	14th Amendment Citizen / Resident / Legal Person
Basis of Standing	Natural allegiance to a sovereign state	Statutory creation under federal and state codes
Rights	Protected by original state constitutions and natural law	Granted and regulated by legislative bodies
Duties	None, unless expressly consented	Mandatory compliance with statutory schemes (e.g., taxes, licenses)
Legal Definitions	Inhabitant, Citizen of a state	Individual, person, taxpayer, resident
Jurisdiction	Common law, organic constitution	Administrative and statutory courts

Territorial Jurisdiction

This chart illustrates how presence and implied consent are used to establish territorial jurisdiction in modern administrative systems. Jurisdiction is not based solely on physical presence, but on conduct that implies consent through participation in federally and state controlled identifiers and benefits via a contractual nexus.

Table 4:

Some Indicators	Interpretation	Effect (Jurisdictional Outcome)
Use of ZIP CODE	Voluntary entry into a federal postal zone	Presumed federal jurisdiction via postal/territorial regulation
Listing Residence in STATE	Consent to domicile in a federal municipal corporation	Subject to statutory and administrative codes
Driver's License / Vehicle Registration	Application for state-granted privileges	Consent to regulation under transportation and traffic codes
Social Security Number (SSN)	Application for federal benefits	Deemed participation in federal programs and subject to related laws
Voter Registration	Agreement to participate in federal/state corporate elections	Waiver of certain standing as a sovereign and acceptance of statutory status
Filing IRS 1040 Form	Consent to status of U.S. taxpayer	Jurisdiction conferred via voluntary tax obligations

Federal Union vs. National Government: Key Distinctions

Federal Union and National Government are fundamentally different in structure, sovereignty, and the source of authority. The original Constitution established a federal union of sovereign states, not a consolidated national government.

Table 5:

Concept	Federal Union (Union of states)	National Government
Source of Sovereignty	Sovereignty resides in the people of each individual state	Sovereignty resides in a single national central authority
Structure	Compact among states; states delegate limited powers to central gov't	Central government is supreme; local governments exist by its permission
Legal Foundation	Constitution is a contract (compact) between states	Constitution is viewed as a supreme charter binding all people directly
Authority Over Citizens	Federal gov't acts on states; states act on Citizens	Central gov't acts directly on individuals, often bypassing state mechanisms
Representation	States are represented as sovereign units (e.g., Senate)	Citizens are represented proportionally (e.g., national popular vote)
Key Historical Model	United States under Articles of Confederation; early U.S. Constitution	Unitary states like France; nationalist movements

Natural Rights, State-Protected Rights, and Federal (14th Amendment) Rights

Table 6:

Category	Natural Rights (Unalienable/ Inalienable)	State-Protected Rights (Original Compact)	Federal Rights (14th Amendment)
Source	Creator / Natural Law	State Constitutions, Common Law	U.S. Constitution (Post-Civil War)
Examples	Life, liberty, property, conscience, movement, defense, religious freedom	Suffrage (right of voting), property rights, trial by jury, religious practice	Due Process, Equal Protection, Incorporation of certain Bill of Rights provisions
Authority to Enforce	Individual conscience, community, common law courts	State courts, legislatures, executive branches	Federal courts, Congress, federal agencies
Can be Waived or Licensed?	No; unalienable by definition	Some may be licensed (e.g., bar practice, voting age requirements)	Yes; most rights may be licensed or waived through statutes, contracts, regulations
Citizen Designation	Man/woman under God; sovereign individual; original state Citizen	Citizen of a state (e.g., Citizen of Virginia)	Citizen of the United States under 14th Amendment
Privileges or Duties	Duties arise from divine law and reason; rights are not conditional	Civic duties like militia service or jury duty	Rights often come with statutory obligations (e.g., taxes, military draft, compliance)

Table 7:

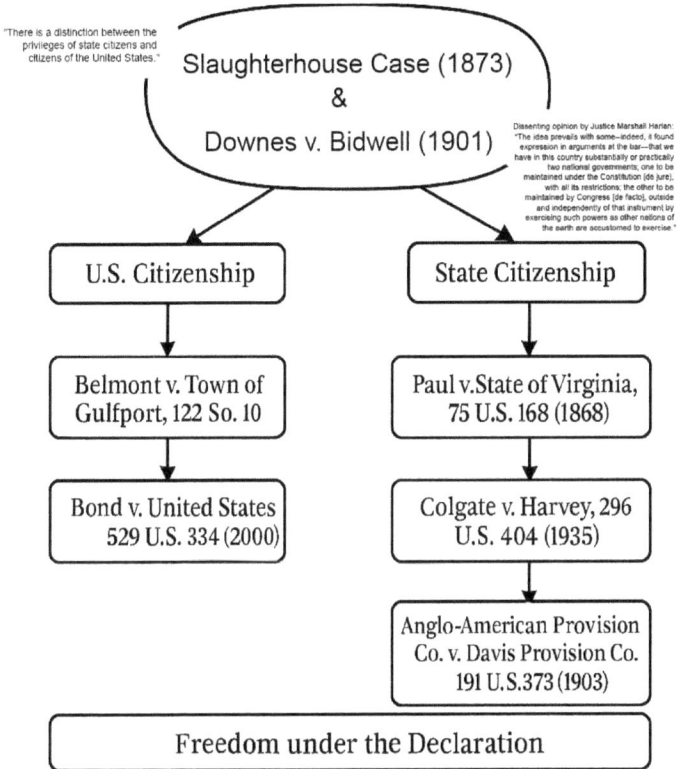

"There is a distinction between the privileges of state citizens and citizens of the United States."

Slaughterhouse Case (1873)
&
Downes v. Bidwell (1901)

Dissenting opinion by Justice Marshall Harlan: "The idea prevails with some—indeed, it found expression in arguments at the bar—that we have in this country substantially or practically two national governments; one to be maintained under the Constitution (de jure), with all its restrictions; the other to be maintained by Congress (de facto), outside and independently of that instrument by exercising such powers as other nations of the earth are accustomed to exercise."

U.S. Citizenship

State Citizenship

Belmont v. Town of Gulfport, 122 So. 10

Paul v. State of Virginia, 75 U.S. 168 (1868)

Bond v. United States 529 U.S. 334 (2000)

Colgate v. Harvey, 296 U.S. 404 (1935)

Anglo-American Provision Co. v. Davis Provision Co. 191 U.S. 373 (1903)

Freedom under the Declaration

About the Authors

Kelby Smith is the Executive Director of HIS Advocates, s.s.m., a private, self-supported, unincorporated ministry committed to educating and empowering individuals to lawfully reclaim their rights as state Citizens. Under his leadership, the ministry has become a trusted source for those seeking to operate outside the jurisdiction of the United States Corporation through private association, lawful processes, and constitutional principles.

HIS Advocates is recognized as a private church ministry and association that provides education and support on state Citizenship, private trusts, asset protection, and financial sovereignty. It also operates as a national TV network and social platform through HISAdvocates.TV, currently available on Roku, Amazon Fire, Apple TV, Android TV, Samsung, LG, mobile apps, YouTube, and more.

A seasoned entrepreneur, licensed real estate broker, educator, and faith-based advocate, Kelby brings over two decades of experience in private finance, legal education, and emerging technologies. Since founding HIS Advocates in 2012, he has built a dynamic national community of individuals transitioning into the private, living beyond the constraints of conventional systems.

In 2020, he launched HISAdvocates.TV, providing podcasters and independent voices a censorship-free media platform. Kelby has produced hundreds of episodes covering topics such as private health coverage, lawful sovereignty, estate planning, and true American history. He is also a sought-after speaker at conferences and workshops across the country.

In his powerful new book, What Does It Mean to Be an American, Kelby challenges readers to reevaluate their understanding of citizenship, allegiance, and constitutional freedom. Blending historical truth, personal experience, and practical strategies, he provides a compelling roadmap to reclaiming one's lawful identity and living as a truly free, informed American.

Kelby Smith
Executive Director
HIS Advocates, s.s.m.
✉ kelby@hisadvocates.org
☎ (844) 447-2386 ext 701
🌐 www.HISAdvocates.org
📺 www.HISAdvocates.TV

Ebiezer, whom many know as Ebie, counts his highest calling as serving God through his private ministries. He is a full-time, stay-at-home husband and father of three sons. He is a U.S. Marine Corps veteran, founder of Kingdom Country Foundation, and director of the Cybersecurity Research Foundation. After joining HIS Advocates in 2018 and completing the Living-in-the-Private Program in 2020, he left his federal government roles where he served as a security and cybersecurity consultant to live privately, lawfully, and faithfully before his Creator.

At HIS Advocates he serves as IT Director, member counselor and special-projects lead. His Bible scholarship and avid legal and historical research empower him and the ministry to guide others in restructuring how they live, work, and serve in alignment with God's Kingdom. For Ebie, State Citizenship is simply a byproduct of a deeper truth: real freedom begins with knowing who you are in God.

His contribution to this book flows from that conviction, rooted in Scripture, reinforced by meticulous study and research of American jurisprudence, and sustained by unwavering faith in our Creator.

Ebiezer,
Ambassador and Witness to Christ.
IT Director
HIS Advocates, s.s.m.
✉ ebie@hisadvocates.org
☎ (844) 447-2386 ext. 2

M arkus's journey began at the age of ten, when the loss of his mother sparked a lifelong quest for truth in a world that often felt upside down. From rebellious teen to relentless seeker, Markus never stopped questioning—driven by a deep desire to understand life's greater purpose. Influenced by his paternal grandmother's unwavering faith in God and the legacy of his maternal grandfather, an Estonian Lutheran Minister who fled Soviet persecution after WWII, Markus came to recognize the quiet strength of God's divine love, always guiding and watching his back.

A rebel at heart and a curious mind by nature, Markus discovered early on that things are rarely as they seem. One book in particular, about lawfully escaping the chains of ignorance-based slavery, struck a deep chord, confirming what he had long suspected. In 1995, that revelation set him on a path to begin "living in the private unofficially."

Over the past three decades, Markus has built a life as a serial entrepreneur, visionary marketer, and best-selling author. Through his work and now as the Executive Director of **OMD Market Research Foundation**, a private, self-supported, unincorporated, humanitarian foundation, he empowers business owners, physicians, and leaders to step into their full abundance, success, and spiritual truth. By combining digital marketing, strategic consulting, and publishing, he helps others build legacies grounded in purpose and prosperity.

In 2024, Markus aligned with HIS Advocates and has since completed nearly 80% of the Living in the Private Program, thrilled to now "officially" live in the private, and even more so, to have brothers who walk that path with him.

Above all, Markus is a devoted father to a daughter who lights up his life and rocks his world, and a grateful man who found the love of his life later in life—an incredible woman who is his best friend, soulmate, and companion on this journey. His contribution to this book is anchored in deep conviction, truth, law, and history—delivered with the kind of knowing that only our Creator can bestow.

"I thank God every day for leading me to Kelby and Ebie. Their teachings have transformed my life in ways they may never fully realize. Glory be!"

Markus "Loving" Ketel
Executive Director
OMD Market Research Foundation
OMDMarketResearchFoundation.org

Notes:

Notes:

Notes:

_____

_____

_____

_____

_____

_____

_____

_____

_____

_____

_____

_____

_____

_____

_____

_____

_____

_____

_____

_____

_____

_____

Notes: